Completely
Toby

A Down Syndrome Story

Justine Green, Ed.D.

illustrated by **Ana Luísa Silva**

Published by

Green Rose Publishing LLC
BOCA RATON, FL

ISBN: Softcover: 9781-7352558-6-6
Ebook: 978-1-7352558-7-3

Illustrations and cover by Ana Luisa Silva

To Tobias, his amazing family, and the Down syndrome community

-JG

Thank you to the Reflections Church BK

-Tobias' Mom, Tamara Mose

Once upon a time,
In a land not so far away...
Justine and Toby lived in a place
Where people were helpful every day.

6

Justine and Toby
Were friends at first peek.
They were silly, fun
And both were unique.

7

Their class was given
A museum tour.
All of the classmates
Would love it for sure.

MUSEUM

MAIL

STOP

9

When they got to the museum
There was so much to see...
Animals of all sizes from
A whale to bumblebee.

While getting the tour
Someone pointed at Toby.

"what's wrong with him?"
They asked so rudely

Toby was having fun.
But his sadness grew
When that boy was mean, Toby became blue.
Toby was blue...

Then turned **red**
and that's when Justine said,
"You are special and true...
You know just what to do"

16

Toby and Justine
Went right over to say,
"Toby has Down syndrome
That's what makes him this way."

You may not understand today,
But Toby is different and that's okay!

Toby might speak differently
And have special features.
He does things his own way and
loves all the earthly creatures.

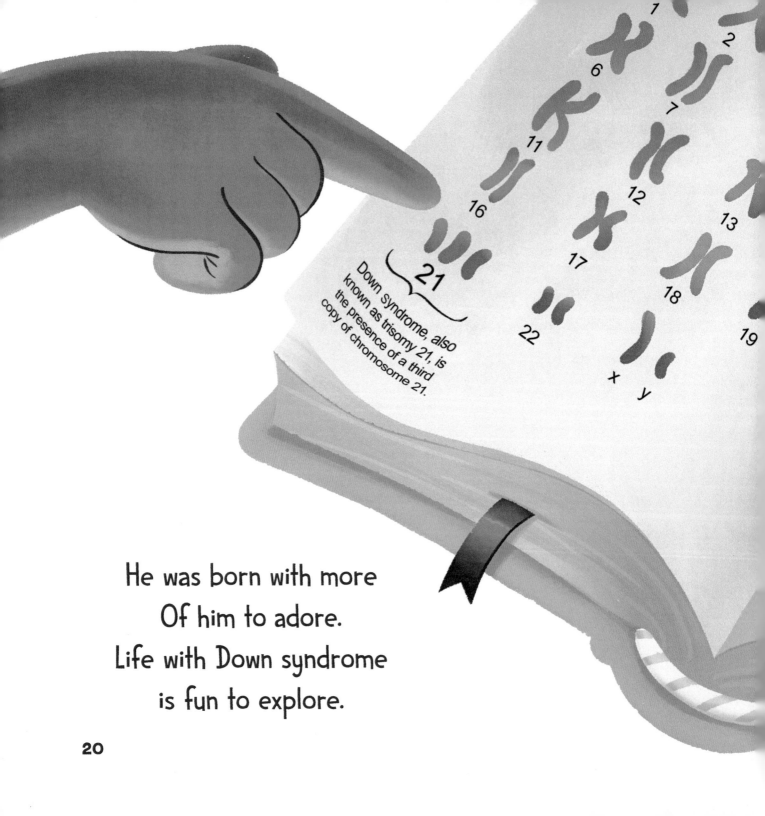

Down Syndrome, also known as trisomy 21, is the presence of a third copy of chromosome 21.

He was born with more
Of him to adore.
Life with Down syndrome
is fun to explore.

4

5

9

10

15

For more information on Down syndrome, please visit NDSS.org

The colors of Down syndrome

Everyone should know that there's
Nothing he can't do!

He may learn and gr**OW**
slowly but he's
Toby through and through.

Toby's Sister

22

23

Toby has Down syndrome
And he has a heart of gold.
Instead, it is **our** hearts
That need to break the mold.

Because everyone is different
And that is true,
You are unique and special...

You are perfect as YOU!

About the Author

Justine Green, Ed.D. is an educator, author, and disability advocate who wrote *Completely Me* based on her own life and coming-of-age journey and is now sharing other children's stories, turning *Completely Me* into a series. She is a five time award-winning author, a member of the Society of Children's Books Writers and Illustrators, and a member of the Independent Book Publishers Association. Justine previously served as a teacher in inclusive classrooms, as a learning specialist, and as the Principal of Tamim Academy in Boca Raton.

Justine earned her Bachelor of Science in Elementary and Special Education from the University of Miami, a Master of Arts from Teachers College, Columbia University and her Doctorate of Education in Higher Education Leadership focusing on students with disabilities. Justine currently resides in Florida with her husband and two children.

About the Illustrator

Ana Luísa Silva is a Portuguese artist specializing in illustration. While she studied audiovisual, multimedia, and 3D animation in college, she is a self-taught illustrator who considers drawing her greatest passion. As a visually-impaired artist with congenital glaucoma, she embodies the *Completely Me* spirit and was able to successfully provide the perfect visual complement to the author's powerful message.

Other Books in the Series

Made in the USA
Coppell, TX
08 October 2024

38357102R00019